Chapter 1

NVC Fundamentals

Non-violent communication is a technique created by Marshall Rosenberg for communicating during conflicts in a way that begins with authentic expression and results in genuine connection.

It's a way of speaking that allows one to express their most uncomfortable feelings while involving no judgements, blame, or accusations and instead encourages the use of facts, feelings, needs and specific requests.

One of the most important and influential parts of life are our relationships and every significant relationship is bound to have conflicts. Disagreements and misunderstandings will occasionally happen, even in the best of circumstances.

During these conflicts, many people will take things personally, get triggered, and lash out in ways they normally wouldn't if they weren't upset. Unless you choose the life of an ascetic, these types of interactions are nearly unavoidable in today's world. Using non-violent communication (NVC) with the proper technique can help to turn every conflict into an opportunity for a deeper connection.

When we are in the midst of a conflict and feel upset, it is often a challenge to tell a loved one we are feeling annoyed, angry, or hurt and have it received in a way in which they don't get defensive or triggered. This is partly because it has become socially acceptable in our culture to criticize, blame, and/or guilt trip whenever we express our displeasure with someone. Throughout the modern world it is commonplace to use indirect, manipulative, and threatening tactics to try to get even our smallest needs met.

Below is an example of a typical interaction using both violent and non-violent communication techniques.

A friend or lover is tapping their foot next to you as you are trying to focus on reading and you are feeling annoyed.

Possible response #1 (violent)

The High Road

Say nothing as annoyance continues to build incrementally until after 20 minutes there is an outburst sounding something like…

"Would you stop? I'm trying to focus!"

The person may stop but there is little chance of the connection level increasing after an outburst like that because each sentence uses a subtly different violent tactic.

Sentence 1. *"Would you stop?"*

This is an example of a demand, disguised as a request.

When we make a demand, what we are truly saying is the other person has to obey our wishes or there will be trouble. If a person cannot say no to a request without punishment, then it is a demand.

Sentence 2. *"I'm trying to focus"*

Guilt Trip

This sentence is implying the other person is to blame for their focusing issues and is therefore *"wrong and bad"* for tapping their foot.

What they really desire is silence so they can focus easier but from an NVC perspective their tactics for achieving this are violent.

Possible response #2 (violent)

> *"Can you please stop tapping your foot? It's really annoying."*

Sentence 1. *"Can you please stop tapping your foot?"*

Another example of a demand disguised as a request

It is designed to sound like a request by throwing in a *"please"* but when viewed with the next sentence it becomes clear it is really a demand. If they don't stop tapping their foot, then some form of trouble will surely ensue is the implication.

A request allows room for alternatives where a path to more dialogue is still an option. A request can be refused without automatically starting a conflict; a demand cannot.

Sentence 2. *"It's really annoying"*

An example of a judgement/criticism.

This sentence is telling them with absolute certainty they are annoying and *"wrong and bad"* for what they are doing. Most people don't react well to being told they are *"wrong and bad."* Communication becomes much harder and fights much easier every single time we judge, accuse, or criticize anyone.

A lot of direct and implied information is included in this one simple sentence;

1. the foot tapping is annoying, **(judgement)**

2. you're a person who does annoying things, **(criticism)**

3. if you don't stop there is going to be trouble. **(Threat)**

It's not a question of: is the judgement correct or not. A judgement can neither be right nor wrong as it is simply an opinion.

When attempting to have an authentic and productive communication, it is good to remember that nobody wants to have their freedom limited or to be criticized and told they are wrong for doing something, being something, or feeling a certain way.

If your communication contains even a hint of these, then your actual message is likely to go unheard. All they will hear is the criticism. Common responses to being criticized are;

Defensiveness

"Well, excuse me for not being a perfect human being!"

Counter Attacking

"Oh yeah? Well, you were being super annoying last night eating with your mouth open but I didn't say anything!"

Shutting Down or withdrawing into a moody silence.

These are all violent tactics meeting violent tactics which leads to more violent communications, arguments, pain and separation. This is exactly what NVC is designed to help with. When you use NVC, you are authentically expressing yourself while getting your needs met without the use of violent tactics.

NVC uses facts, feelings, needs, and requests. It leaves out evaluations, judgements, criticisms, analysis, advice, accusations, and opinions. This is because when trying to work out a conflict these tactics inevitably do more harm than good.

Using the previous foot tapping scenario as can example, a non-violent communication might sound something like this;

Possible response #3 (nonviolent)

"You're tapping your foot and I'm feeling annoyed because I would like silence to focus right now. Would you be willing to stop or go into the other room?"

Clean and authentic without a hint of judgement. Let's examine it closer.

Sentence 1a *"You're tapping your foot."*

Nothing but an observable **FACT**. It's hard to be offended or defensive when someone points out an indisputable fact. (though certainly not impossible)

Sentence 1b *"I'm feeling annoyed"*

This sentence expresses how they are authentically **FEELING** while blaming no one and simply stating it as a fact. Facts are neutral. Saying *"It's annoying* *me"* or *"you're annoying me"* are evaluations of what is going on and they both imply the other person is annoying aka "wrong and bad". *"I feel annoyed,"* is just neutral information. No implications of wrongdoing by anyone, no hidden judgements or guilt trips; just an honest statement about what is alive in them in the present moment.

Expressing how we feel also tends to bring an instant feeling of connection because it shows vulnerability to admit what we are genuinely experiencing in the moment. When our words match the energy we are putting off, it resonates and trust and connection build.

Sentence 1c *"I would like silence to focus right now."*

This part explains WHY they are feeling annoyed by highlighting what need or desire of theirs isn't being met.

This step is very important and easy to overlook. When we express why we feel the way we do, the other person will have a much easier time understanding where we are coming from and will be more likely to want to help us get our needs met. It's easier for them to empathize with us because we are being honest and clear with no hidden judgements or guilt trips that imply they are *"wrong and bad."*

The moment someone hears or senses a hidden implication they are *"wrong and bad"* it becomes much harder for them to really hear, remember, or care what your needs are anymore because they will tend to want to defend themselves.

Sentence 2. *"Would you be willing to stop or go into the other room?"*

This is an example of a specific and doable REQUEST as opposed to a demand which leaves little to no room for discussion. It is also not a vague and general request like-*"Could you be more considerate?"* or *"Would you be willing to be more respectful?*

You can't measure how considerate or respectful someone is, so there is a lack of clarity which is only going to postpone the resolution of the conflict. In the above request both options (*"to go into the other room or stop"*) will be immediately known with certainty.

These are the fundamental principles of **NVC**. Point out a **FACT**, express how you **FEEL,** express **WHY** you feel this way by naming what need or desire isn't being met, and end with a specific and achievable **REQUEST,** without implying the other person is wrong or bad.

FACT FEELING WHY REQUEST

It's a relatively simple technique yet it requires effort to implement because it involves a rewiring of how most of us have been taught to communicate our whole lives.

At first it may feel awkward as you try to speak with no evaluations, judgements, or analysis; instead using facts, feelings and requests, especially if you try it in a moment of tension. With consistent, well intentioned practice, it can become second nature and deepen and enliven every single one of your relationships for the rest of your life.

Chapter 2

Getting Started

The preliminary step to successful communications using NVC is becoming aware of and accepting how we feel in our bodies, especially when it is unpleasant or painful. Once we are in touch with how we feel, we have something genuine to communicate.

When conflicts arise, they usually begin when we or another person have a feeling other than joy in ourselves. These feelings arise for a reason and give us information on how our environment, actions and thoughts are affecting our life. They will not disappear until expressed in some form, and this is why it is so important to communicate.

Before I learned NVC I would often judge myself if I felt sad, annoyed or angry as if I was doing something wrong by feeling this way. As if it was bad or spiritually immature to feel things like anger, irritation, sadness, awkwardness or embarrassment.

Through NVC I have learned that all emotions and feelings are valid and they arise to guide us back towards joy. Negative emotions let us know when something is not in alignment with our world and our higher selves. They give us information that may not always feel pleasant in the moment, but will always bring clarity and inspiration for how to take action toward improving our life if we take the time to listen.

If we didn't have feelings, we wouldn't know what we like or don't like. We would be like robots with intelligence and free will, but no preference because everything would result in the same state of non-feeling.

We learn and grow in life through feelings and emotions, especially the painful, uncomfortable ones. Suppressing or ignoring them cuts us off from one of our greatest sources of information and inspiration. Listening to them, accepting them unconditionally, and expressing them in an authentic productive way gives us full access to the enormous power and potential of the human experience.

No one is wrong or bad for how they feel because no one has direct control of their emotions. People can't just decide to feel excited, bored, happy, or overwhelmed.

For example, if your musician friend is playing you their new song and it bores you while you listen, it doesn't mean you are wrong or shallow or they are not good musicians. Those would be assumptions and judgements. It just means you felt bored when you listened to them play their song and this could be for several reasons. Maybe you don't resonate with the style of music, maybe you were not in the mood to hear music, maybe the lyrics were not interesting to you. The truth is you felt bored.

If you pretend you like it when you really don't then authenticity will lessen between the two of you and the interaction will lack the excitement of a genuine communication. If you are honest with them, even though it might be painful at first, you are giving them useful information which in the long run will be a lot more helpful to them in understanding how their music affects people and thus their career.

If the musician shows his song to 10 people and they all pretend they like it, the musician might be happier in that moment but it probably won't help him create music that resonates with people. If 9 out of the 10 people honestly inform him the song is not resonating with them, it is likely to feel more painful for him but also much more beneficial to his long-term success. Which would you prefer if you were the musician?

If you wake up one morning feeling depressed it doesn't mean you are wrong, sick, or bad at life and it's not something to be avoided at all costs. It doesn't mean you should beat yourself up and judge yourself for feeling this way. It just means your soul is telling you something about the way you are living your life in the only way it can, through feelings and emotions; the language of the soul.

You can run from unpleasant emotions like depression and sadness for a while but it is not a sustainable tactic. It is much more productive to accept how you feel in a nonjudgmental way and know there is a valid reason for this feeling arising. It is not some type of mistake or malfunction. If you put nonjudgemental attention on the feeling in your body long enough, it will let you know exactly what you need to do to get back to happiness.

Feel the pain, even when you don't understand it intellectually. It will eventually pass and leave behind inspiration and joy; this is the process. Ignoring or suppressing pain only brings more pain until it becomes so powerful it's impossible to ignore.

If we are alone, expressing our emotions might mean quietly putting nonjudgmental attention on the feelings in our body. The feelings want your attention so they can be heard and pass on important information to you regardless of if they are pain, happiness, sadness, dread, annoyance, joy etc.

Their sole purpose is to give you information about this journey of life and they won't move on until they achieve that. Emotional pain may be the greatest teacher mankind has.

Even if we continually avoid and suppress an unpleasant emotion it doesn't disappear. The energy of that emotion just gets stored somewhere in your body and waits for a chance to get your attention. While it is stored it represents a blockage energetically which can lead to a variety of mental, emotional and/or physical illnesses. Eventually, after continually repressing and avoiding enough emotions we create what Eckhart Tolle calls the "pain body."

I like to think of the pain body as a group of suppressed emotions waiting for a chance to fulfill their purpose and share their message with us. The pain body is not our enemy, it's one of our greatest friends that has been mistreated and ignored for a long time and needs attention.

If the feeling we repressed was annoyance then it will group together with other similar repressed feelings of annoyance still lingering in our energetic field and together they wait for their chance to be heard. Their chance comes when similar feelings arise in the person in the present moment.

This is why we sometimes drastically overreact to minor things. Instead of an incident being mildly irritating something can feel intensely frustrating because of all the old suppressed emotions trying to come out at once and be expressed.

If we express our anger in a sudden outburst, this will release some of the backlog of repressed stagnant energy. This is why it often feels good to do so. The danger is it also tends to create excessive disharmony in our environment, our social world and our bodies. A much gentler and effective way to release these repressed emotions is to simply allow them to have some of your attention when they arise.

We don't need to figure them out intellectually or think about them to release them from our bodies. Simply using gentle, nonjudgmental attention on where we have the feeling in our bodies can quickly turn these negative and uncomfortable feelings into joy and clarity. If we are alone, this can be a private and silent exercise. If we are not alone, it may mean letting another know how we feel and this is where NVC comes in.

CHAPTER 3

Facts VS Evaluations

After the preliminary process of accepting and honoring how we feel, the next step is pointing out what is bothering us by using only observable facts with no evaluations. Evaluations are unnecessary when using NVC because they often imply that someone is at fault which can then lead to defensiveness and a breakdown in communication.

For example

"Your room is a mess" is an evaluation while, *"Your bed is unmade, there are dirty clothes on the floor, and you have a pile of trash in the corner"* are all observable facts.

Essentially, they both convey the same message except one also implies that the person is *"wrong and bad"* for having a messy room and the other is simply pointing out observable facts with no implied judgements.

Remember, as soon as we imply someone is *"wrong or bad"* the chances of them getting triggered increase exponentially while the chances of our needs getting met without a fight go down exponentially.

"You're driving recklessly" is an evaluation while, *"you're driving 20 miles over the speed limit and you just ran that red light,"* are facts.

Speaking with facts is not about being nice, it's about being authentic and effective. Even if 100 out of 100 people would agree that the room is messy, and the person is driving recklessly, it is still just an opinion AKA judgement and stating it out loud will likely be received as they are *"wrong and bad"* making it harder to communicate. Here are some additional examples

"You're drunk" -evaluation.

"I smell alcohol on your breath and you are slurring your words"-observable facts

"You don't care about your job"-evaluation

"You have been late to work every day this week"-observable fact

"You're being disrespectful" -evaluation.

"You have interrupted me three times in a row." -observable fact

It is essential to get a good grasp of this concept or your attempts at using NVC will often backfire. The goal is to speak only in observable facts and avoid all evaluations.

The instant we imply someone is *"wrong and bad"* they are likely to become triggered and defensive. As soon as they are triggered, communication is compromised. The beauty of NVC is that when used correctly it enables you to authentically communicate your negative or uncomfortable truths without giving someone an easy reason to get triggered because it never implies they are in the wrong.

Sometimes, even though you are using proper NVC, people will still get triggered and lash out. When this happens, it is best to use one of the most amazing, simple and powerful tools in NVC; Emergency Empathy, which will be explained in greater detail later in chapter 7.

In summary, the first step is to point out an observable fact with no hint of a judgement, evaluation, or condemnation and without any implications that anyone is wrong, bad or to blame. The goal is to simply point out a neutral and observable fact which will set the ground for the rest of the communication process.

Chapter 4

Feelings and Accountability

A core principle of NVC is taking responsibility for how we feel regardless of the circumstances. No matter what has happened, we are all responsible for how we feel one hundred percent of the time. How we feel is a direct reflection of our thoughts. Change your perspective about an incident and you will change how you feel.

This can be another challenging concept at first but it is essential for effective communication to occur. As soon as we blame other people for our inner state, we are again implying that they are *"bad and wrong"* and we are a victim of their wrongdoings and then communication will quickly deteriorate.

No matter what has happened it is always up to us how we react to a situation. We react based on how we feel and our feelings are based on our thoughts and beliefs. Every time you change your perception, you will change how you feel and since you are the only person who can change your thoughts and perceptions, you are the only person ultimately responsible for how you feel.

Admittedly, other people can make things much easier or harder for our inner state depending on how they act but the reality is they are little more than a stimulus for our positive or negative reactions.

If we get stood up on a date we might feel angry, sad, relieved, hurt, embarrassed or any number of ways but they all depend first on our expectations and not the actual incident. We may feel one way at first, think about it for a minute and then feel a different way. It's completely up to us and therefore it would not be accurate to blame someone else even though they were the person who stood us up.

This doesn't mean that we let people take advantage of us and become a doormat to everyone. On the contrary, I recommend not allowing people to treat you in any way you do not wish to be treated which is why NVC gives you the tools to communicate your needs and set clear boundaries without playing the victim.

If we live with the attitude that we are responsible for our emotional state, then we can avoid feeling like a victim to how other people and the world treat us. If we believe other people control how we feel then we will be constantly at the mercy of everything around us.

In relationships people often say things like,

"you're annoying me, that really hurt my feelings, you're pissing me off, you're driving me crazy." etc

All of these statements are implying that they are a victim to another's actions, they are not responsible for how they feel, and the other person is *"wrong and bad"* again for making them feel so unpleasant.

For example, say your friend borrowed your car and crashed it. Depending on your perspective you might be furious, or you might be relieved that your friend is ok. You might feel guilty that you loaned them the car or you might be happy that you have full coverage and can get a new car. The incident is neutral; you are the one that puts the meaning into it which will then affect how you feel.

This is how we approach the second step in a non-violent communication as we express how we are feeling. We accept it, own it and express it in a neutral, authentic way. If we imply the other person is responsible for how we feel then communication will break down. This is not about being nice, or mean, it's about being honest, effective, and impeccable with our word.

Imagine someone is saying the following statements to you and see if you feel any difference.

"*I feel annoyed*" (owning it) as opposed to "*you're annoying me*". (Blaming)

"*I'm angry*" (owning it) as opposed to "*you're making me angry*". (Blaming)

"*I feel hurt*" (owning it) as opposed to "*you hurt my feelings*". (Blaming)

"*I feel sad*" (owning it) as opposed to "*you are making me sad*" (blaming)

When the feeling is owned and expressed as a fact, it's much easier for the person you are speaking with to continue listening and hear what you are really saying. When we blame someone else for our pain, most of the time they will feel at least a little triggered or defensive and communication will again break down.

In summary, first we accept and honor that we have an undesirable feeling in ourselves, second we use observable facts to point out what has happened that is contributing to this feeling, and third we state how we feel authentically and in such a way that blames no one else for its occurrence.

****

A common misstep here is to start your sentence with, *"I feel as if...,"* or *"I feel like"*... These intros inevitably lead to an evaluation, analysis, or criticism and not an actual feeling.

For example, *"I feel like you are not listening to me"* is an evaluation, not a feeling, and it implies the other person is *"wrong and bad"* for not listening to you. Frustration or anger might be the actual feeling they were trying to express.

"I feel as if you don't care about me" is again, not a feeling but an evaluation implying more wrongdoing. The underlying message/guilt trip being *"you should care more about me but you don't so you're bad and wrong and I'm a victim."* Sadness or loneliness might be the actual feeling in this case.

These are both evaluations and criticisms disguised as feelings and again nearly every person I have ever worked with falls into this trap in their beginning attempts at NVC. A feeling is usually one word. If you find yourself using more than one word to describe how you feel that's a good sign you are actually expressing an evaluation/judgement/criticism and not a feeling.

"I feel sad, I feel angry, I feel disgusted, I feel lonely, I feel enraged," etc. These are proper NVC statements about how one feels; short and to the point. They contain no judgements and no implications of the other person being responsible; just honest expressions of what emotions are currently alive inside of them.

The reason this is such a common misstep is that it is much easier to blame someone else for how we feel than to admit how we feel and take full responsibility for it. Saying, *"I feel angry"* takes courage, saying *"you are pissing me off"* takes much less.

Another common misstep is to use words that imply something was done to you like, "*I feel disrespected, I feel betrayed, I feel abused, I feel mistreated, I feel unappreciated*" etc. These too are all evaluations disguised as feelings and they imply that the other person has done you wrong and you again are a victim to their injustice; the opposite of NVC.

As a general guideline, stay away from verbs that imply somebody doing something to you when describing how you feel. Some more examples of words to avoid when describing your feelings are *tricked, ambushed, bullied, provoked, terrorized, insulted, criticized, abandoned, disrespected, ignored, abused* etc.

This is where it can sometimes get tricky and there are some definite gray areas so just keep at it even if you make a lot of mistakes. Focus on keeping your feeling statements short and simple and it can be very helpful to spend time studying the included list of feelings at the end of this book to expand your feelings vocabulary.

Unmet Needs

The third step in NVC is to authentically express why you feel the way you do. It's the step where you define what needs you have that are not being met or what desires you have that in your opinion, would make life better.

Behind every unpleasant feeling, is an unmet need/desire. It could be a need for safety, for cleanliness, for peace, for connection, for freedom, for conversation, for reliability, to be heard, etc. The list is endless. The unmet need is why you are upset and not whatever incident has occurred. The incident is neutral and up to interpretation by everyone involved but your needs are specific. It is a subtle but powerful distinction.

For instance, say you are riding with someone who is speeding and you feel upset because you have a desire for safety. If you say, *"I'm feeling really anxious* **(feeling)** *because you're driving recklessly,"* **(judgement)** you have blamed them for your inner state and implied they are *"bad and wrong."* This is not likely to go well.

If you say, *"I'm feeling really anxious* **(feeling)** *because I value my safety,"* **(need)** you have just communicated nonjudgemental and accurate information that is much easier to digest.

Another example could be that someone keeps interrupting you and you feel annoyed because of your need to be heard or your desire for good manners. If you say, *"you keep interrupting me* **(fact)** *and it's annoying,"* **(judgement)** you are blaming them and implying they are *"bad and wrong"*.

If you say, *"you keep interrupting me* **(fact)** *and I'm feeling annoyed* **(feeling)** *because I would like to be heard,"* **(need)** it is much more likely to be received in a productive way and is also more accurate and honest.

It is fairly easy to leave this step out, but it's just as important as every other step and is essential to consistent successful NVC communications.

Explore the difference between these two statements from a couple roommates.

"There are dirty dishes from your dinner last night in the sink and I'm feeling angry."

These are the first two steps done properly of NVC (**observable fact** and a **feeling**), yet without the third step, the message is unclear. It could easily be interpreted as them implying the other person is *"wrong and bad"* for leaving the dirty dishes and is responsible for their current anger. This is not likely to lead to an easy and productive communication.

Once the third step is added, things become much more clear and easier to hear.

"There are dirty dishes from your dinner last night in the sink **(fact)** *and I'm feeling angry* **(feeling)** *because having a clean kitchen is really important to me."* **(need)**

They clearly state that they are angry because *"a clean kitchen is really important to me."* They are not implying they are angry because the other person is messy AKA *"wrong and bad"*, or responsible for creating their feelings. Instead, they are simply informing them of what is going on inside themselves and why they feel the way they do.

When we use NVC, the goal is to get our needs met while creating more understanding and connection for all involved parties. It is about uncovering the core issue of a conflict and finding a win win solution for everyone from a place of clarity.

****

Often in the heat of the moment, it can be a challenge to put our finger on exactly why we feel the way we do. When anger, annoyance, or any other feeling besides joy arises, they don't always have a clear cause and can appear from out of nowhere, oftentimes with a lot of intensity. This is where practicing NVC helps. The more you practice the more you will become self aware. It is ok to make mistakes and speak slowly as you are integrating this new skill. Take your time.

If you know ahead of time you want to use NVC with someone about a specific issue, practice what you want to say before you meet. Think about what your actual unmet needs are. Articulate what the facts are and practice saying them without implying the other person is somehow responsible. It can often make a world of difference.

****

In summary, we are always responsible for how we feel and it is not helpful to the communication process to imply otherwise.

We feel the way we do based on our thoughts and beliefs about what is appropriate, what is acceptable, and what is expected within the framework of our own belief system.

Every unpleasant feeling represents an unmet need or desire and it's up to us to figure out what it is so we can express it in an attempt to get that need met.

A common misstep at this juncture is to throw in a judgement or criticism without realizing it.

For example

"There are dirty dishes in the sink from last night (fact) and I'm feeling angry (feeling) because I value not living with messy people," **(judgement)** is not NVC. An indirect insult is still an insult and as soon as you call someone messy they are likely to get triggered and defensive.

Another example is

"When you showed up late to our meeting (fact) I felt angry (feeling) because I don't like people wasting my time." **(guilt trip)**

The first two parts are proper NVC but the third part implies that the other person wastes people's time, possibly on purpose and possibly chronically. AKA they are *"wrong and bad"*

Using NVC it might sound like this;

"When you showed up late to our meeting, (fact) I felt angry (feeling) because my time is very important to me..."

No judgements or indirect insults in there anywhere; just facts, feelings, and an explanation as to why they feel as they do.

To do NVC effectively it is important to be in touch with what need we have that is not being met. Until we can do that, whatever dispute we are in is not likely to be permanently resolved.

Once both people can identify and verbalize what unmet needs they have, a resolution is usually not far away. It can also be very helpful to repeat back to each other what the other person's needs are once you understand them and vice versa. A lot of connection will build when this happens and finding a win win solution will be much easier.

Chapter 6

Specific Requests

One goal of NVC is to resolve issues so completely they don't have to be revisited again and again. Many long term relationships are still having the same arguments they did in their beginning because they have never uncovered the core issues.

Whatever the challenge is between two people there is always a way to resolve it through revealing the actual needs of both parties. Sometimes the newfound clarity will shed light on something that is a true deal breaker for the relationship and will lead to permanent separation and sometimes it doesn't.

Either way, NVC done properly will eventually get to the root of the issue so both parties can make an informed decision based on their needs and not from a place of being triggered and defensive.

This is where step four comes in. All the other steps have paved the way to the crucial moment of the **Specific and Doable Request**. This is when you have the greatest chance of actually getting what you are looking for and when done correctly it quickly reveals any core issues.

This step, like all the others is relatively simple, yet getting it wrong is very easily done. Vigilance and presence are required every step of the way when using NVC.

A specific and achievable request is something that can be done in a quantifiable way. *"Would you be willing to be more respectful?"* may sound like a reasonable request but how can it be measured? How will anyone know if they are being more respectful, less respectful, or the same amount of respectful? It can't accurately be measured so the request doesn't really mean anything and most likely won't solve whatever the actual issue is. The person can just say yes to pacify the moment and not change a thing until the problem is brought up again at a later date.

For example, Theo and Mary are a married couple having an issue surrounding Theo's money spending habits. If Mary does all the proper NVC steps...

(step 1-fact)"Honey, I saw that our joint account is overdrawn again from the lawn mower you just bought (step 2-feeling) and I'm feeling very anxious (step 3-need) because I really desire more financial stability" ...

but ends with a vague and unquantifiable request like,

"Would you be willing to be more careful with how you spend our money?"

Than she has not really achieved anything except bringing awareness to an issue. Theo can just say yes, end the discussion and then go back to exactly what he was doing before with relative impunity because being more careful is not specific enough to be measurable.

In this case a specific request might be something along the lines of,

"Would you be willing to write down everything you spend money on for the next two weeks?"

Or *"Would you be willing to let me know when you are going to make a purchase of over $100?"*

or *"Would you be willing to only use one account so we can keep track of your spending habits?"*

Each of those requests are measurable and achievable. If they are done or not will be very easy to see. This is the first major point of consideration when making a request. Make sure it is doable and quantifiable.

Another example of an unachievable request could be something like *"Would you be willing to not lose your temper anymore?"* Though someone may truly desire to never lose their temper again it's not something that is in the realm of possibility because that's not how human life works. We may as well be requesting that they become perfect in every way. No one can predict their future emotional states. Real change comes from consistently working on oneself and often takes time.

A more achievable request for this example could be something like,

"Would you be willing to......

"take an anger management class",

"see a therapist,"

or *"read a specific book on anger?"*

These are all specific requests that can easily be seen if they are done or not.

****

Another extremely important consideration is making sure it is a request and not a demand. This really comes down to intention because even if the request is worded correctly according to NVC principles it can still be a demand.

A demand is nothing short of a threat implying *"do what I ask or you will regret it."* If a person cannot refuse your request without some form of punishment be it verbal, emotional, or physical then it is a demand and not a request.

It's not about getting our specific requests met, it's about getting our needs met. There is a difference. The requests are just possible strategies to meet our needs. If Theo refuses her request but comes up with an alternative that still meets her needs, than that is just as good as him agreeing to her original request.

If our only goal in using NVC is to get a specific request met, then we are likely making demands instead of using NVC. In the case of Theo and Mary, if Theo says no because it restricts his need for autonomy and Mary reacts in anger, then it was really a demand all along. If she is open to hearing another solution that could meet her need for financial stability and his need for autonomy, they are then having a proper NVC exchange. She proposed a solution to a need she has and he is offering an alternative. It is perfectly ok to refuse a request and continue looking for another way to meet everyone's needs.

****

Another core principle of NVC is to never compromise. The goal is to get everyone's needs met completely, not just a little. If it feels like a compromise, keep communicating until another solution is found that feels like a win win. This may take more time but in the long run it will be well worth the effort. Go deeper into defining and clarifying what the core needs are for both parties until neither feels like they are compromising.

Sometimes you may find yourself getting to the specific request part of the NVC process but feel unsure of what you want to ask. This could possibly mean a few different things.

Maybe you just really wanted to be heard so your specific request could be for them to repeat back what you have expressed to them. Maybe you want to know if they are willing to talk about what you have just expressed. The requests don't need to be something big and profound.

However, not knowing what to request may also be a sign that you are not really sure what you want and some further introspection may be required on your part. Just remember this is an incredibly powerful and rewarding technique and mistakes will be made. Be easy on yourself and stay consistent.

Another common mistake I see is that people will leap straight into the request without doing the previous steps. While this sometimes works, it is not a method that tends to build as much connection as following all the steps. Each step builds upon the next to create more connection and understanding so that by the time the specific request comes there is already a momentum built with empathy and clarity.

****

In summary, a **request** is something that can be refused without punishment and is also measurable and doable. If agreeing to someone's request feels like a compromise, keep looking for alternative solutions until you find one that feels like a win win for all parties involved.

Chapter 7

Emergency Empathy

So you've gotten all the steps down and are using NVC like a natural. Nowhere in your statements are you implying anyone else is *"wrong or bad."* You are owning your feelings, expressing them clearly, and have accurately identified your unmet needs as well as a specific request.

Your tone is calm and soothing and you are feeling absolutely great about your new NVC skills. But wait, the person you are talking to is still getting triggered and defensive! That's not supposed to happen. They are even calling you names and blaming you for everything that's going wrong. This isn't how it's supposed to go!

So you take a breath, and then calmly and patiently try again with even better technique and a softer tone…. yet it still doesn't help. In fact, it seems like it's making it worse! You are using all the proper steps and they are using none! This can be a very frustrating experience and one you are likely to come across every so often in your NVC adventures.

Fortunately for us all, there is a solution and it's called, **Emergency Empathy.**

When I was first learning NVC I had two female roommates Liza and Imani, who were having a tough time getting along. It often seemed they had declared war on each other and since one was moving out in a week, they had no interest in even attempting to resolve their issues. It was getting downright ugly. Hearing their vicious arguments was becoming more and more commonplace.

I personally liked them both and was feeling so confident in NVC and my understanding of it, I offered to help mediate their dispute, which they both at separate times unequivocally refused with some choice non NVC words thrown in for good measure. Nevertheless, a moment came when we were all in the kitchen together and tensions were high.

I immediately seized the opportunity to apply NVC and attempted to uncover what their core unmet needs were. For about a minute it looked like I was succeeding. Liza was somewhat calmly explaining some of the issues she had with how Imani carried herself and Imani was calmly listening, right up until she wasn't.

Liza brought up a past incident, Imani got triggered and started defending herself while immediately hurling out insults and accusations at Liza. Liza hurled her own insults and accusations right back at Imani except she also added threats which Imani quickly reciprocated.

It got so intense so fast that I thought physical violence was about to break out before Imani ran into her room and locked the door, screaming threats and insults the whole way. Liza followed suit to her room with some of her own delicately phrased insults and threats and I was left in the kitchen feeling traumatized and ashamed at the results of my first attempts at NVC based mediation.

What did I do wrong? I had repeatedly used all four steps correctly but I also had rapidly made the situation ten times worse. Before then, they had only argued but after my attempt to help they were threatening violence, police and law suits on each other. I was very frustrated and went right back to Marshall Rosenberg's book and quickly realized where I had gone wrong. I had completely forgotten about Emergency Empathy; one of the most powerful tools in NVC for creating connection and de-escalating a potential conflict.

Emergency Empathy is what you use the moment things start to get out of hand. It's what you use the moment you feel like you are in an argument instead of a discussion, when you feel triggered or want to defend yourself, when you realize they are not hearing anything you say or vice versa, the moment you want to prove how right you are and how obviously misinformed the person you are talking to is. These are the key moments to use **Emergency Empathy.**

The challenge is, it's such a simple and powerful tool that it is extremely easy to forget, especially in the heat of the moment.

So without any further ado...

Emergency Empathy is when you guess how someone feels and why they feel as they do.

I know it may sound too simple to be as powerful as I'm suggesting, but when used correctly it literally feels like having a super power. And to top it off, you don't even have to be correct for it to work.

When you genuinely attempt to guess how someone is feeling inside their body, it is a direct and powerful way of connecting with what is alive in them in the present moment. It inevitably feels good to whomever you use it on because it instantly shows that you value what is authentically happening inside of them.

It is also asking someone about one of their favorite subjects, themselves! And it's a subject they know more about than anyone else in the world so they are usually very eager to share their insights with you.

When you couple that with guessing why they feel the way they do, it shows that you are genuinely trying to understand what's going on with them. This will cause them to look inside themselves and see if what you said was correct or not.

Putting our attention inside ourselves is almost always going to have a slightly calming effect on a person. Many meditation styles use this as their fundamental technique because of its immediate and powerful tendency to bring more presence and peace to the meditator.

When you apply Emergency Empathy, most people will stop whatever they were going on about and check in with themselves to correct you with oftentimes very useful information.

So you do another round of Emergency Empathy using the new information they gave you. Again, you may be wrong and they will likely supply you with more information on how they feel and why, all the while becoming less agitated. Every time you use Emergency Empathy it will generally take the intensity of the situation from 100-85, and then 85-70, and then 70-65 and so on.

Eventually, usually after about three rounds of this in my experience, you get it right or close enough to right and they'll say "Yes! I feel hurt because I don't like being ignored!" or "Yes I'm angry because I'm the only one who cleans and no-one ever thanks me!" etc. All of a sudden they feel heard and understood. They are calmer and much more likely to be able to resume an actual conversation instead of a fight. This is when you can go back to using NVC.

Had I used Emergency Empathy in the case of Imani and Liza, I would have been able to help keep the intensity level from exploding into threats of violence. Instead I repeatedly tried to use the four steps despite the fact they weren't working and only ended up making things worse.

If I could go back in time as soon as Imani got triggered it might have sounded like this,...

Step 1-guess how she feels *"Imani, are you feeling angry* (**Step 2-guess why she feels the way she does)** *because you think Liza is leaving out important details?"*

I would have listened to whatever her reply was and depending on her response said something like, *"Ok, so you're feeling frustrated because you don't feel appreciated for all the things you do around the house?"*

I would have kept doing this until Imani felt calm and understood, and then I would have asked her if she would be willing to hear what Liza had to say. If she felt sufficiently heard and understood then she would have no problem letting Liza speak.

I would have kept doing this every time it started to get out of hand with either woman until we uncovered what the actual core reason for their conflict was. Marshall Rosenberg states in his book that it generally takes less than twenty minutes to solve any conflict once the actual unmet needs are uncovered of both parties, and I agree.

There are several reasons why Emergency Empathy is so effective. As a general rule people love being asked about things they know the answer to, they love being asked about themselves, and they love feeling like someone is trying to understand where they are coming from.

All of these things can help make a person feel calm and understood. When we feel calm and understood we don't feel triggered, argumentative, or defensive and therefore are able to have a rational conversation.

In the middle of a fight we feel tense, combative, angry, etc. It very easy to dismiss whatever anyone is saying to you and just continue trying to make your point. Emergency Empathy done properly can cut through all that and instantly take the aggression level down several notches. Every notch the fight intensity level goes down, the potential for a productive communication goes up.

There is little to no benefit of fighting or arguing with anyone, especially someone who you love dearly. Yet somehow the people we love the most tend to trigger us the most. Emergency Empathy is like a magical tool to avoid ever getting into pointless unproductive arguments as long as we can remember to apply it in the heat of the moment.

Let's look at another example. John is well versed in NVC and is using it to communicate to his wife Judy.

John

"Baby, when you use curse words and raise your voice like you just did, (fact) I feel anxious (feeling) because I really value calm, heart centered communication. (need) Would you be willing to lower your voice as we talk?" **(request)**

Judy

"There you go again! Always trying to control me! Why can't you just accept me? I'm so sick of this! You're such a control freak!"

Let's look at Johns options. He can make another attempt at an NVC statement but it is unlikely to bring a different result since the first one didn't work at all even though he used all the four NVC steps correctly. He can defend himself and explain that he is not trying to control her but again she is already triggered and is probably not going to hear anything he says. He can take her statement personally, get mad and start fighting with her using his own accusations, which obviously is not what anyone wants, or he can use **Emergency Empathy** (guess how she feels and why) which might sound something like this.

John

(Round 1)

"Are you upset because you don't think I accept you for who you really are?"

Judy

"No, I'm pissed off because I'm tired of you constantly trying to control me!"

John

(Round 2)

"Ok, so you're saying you're pissed because you think I am trying to control you right now?"

Judy

"No!, I'm sick and tired of not being appreciated for who I am! I don't want to be calm and quiet! I'm not a little church mouse! "

John

(Round 3)

"So you're upset because you don't think I love and appreciate you for who you really are?"

Judy

"Well do you?"

John

"Baby, I hate quiet little church mice!"

Maybe they laugh a little right then but most importantly the energy between them has calmed down with each round of Emergency Empathy he applied. It's no longer a fight where no one is listening and they are just talking over each other with an adversarial energy.

At this point John can attempt another round of NVC and they have a much better chance of actually uncovering the root of whatever the initial issue was. This is the power of **Emergency Empathy**. It allows you to quickly diffuse the combative energy while still remaining authentic and true to yourself.

John didn't lie or apologize or even agree with her accusations. He just took the time to make sure he understood where she was coming from and that was enough to bring the intensity level back down to a normal conversational level.

Despite its power and simplicity there can be many challenges to applying emergency empathy. First off, when we are triggered the last thing we want to do is be rational and understanding. All the ego wants to do is generally show whoever we are arguing with how wrong they are and how right we are. **Emergency Empathy** requires us to step out of the Ego paradigm and focus on the inner world of whom we are talking.

It also requires us to not take personally whatever insults are being thrown at us. This can be particularly challenging but is crucial to using Emergency Empathy successfully.

To me it feels like a Martial Art, but I like to call it a Marshall Art after Marshall Rosenberg, the creator of NVC. When someone hurls an insult, criticism, or judgement at us it's similar to a strike that needs to be dodged. And then instead of returning their attack with our own attack we return it with Emergency Empathy by asking ourselves why would someone feel the need to say that to me and then giving them our best guess.

"Are you angry because you think I did that on purpose?" Or *"Are you upset because you think I don't care about your needs?"* Or *"Are you hurt because you would like more appreciation for what you bring to the table?"*

Instead of attempting to hurt them we are softening them, loving them, extending our presence to them and attempting to connect with what is real inside of them.

Instead of reacting by defending, explaining, analyzing, or counter attacking, just immediately go into Emergency Empathy until the combative energy has settled and connection has increased.

In the beginning of me learning about NVC I would completely forget about Emergency Empathy when I got triggered. It wouldn't be until after the conflict that I would realize I could have used it and had much better results.

Then even when I would remember it, I wouldn't really want to use it because I was generally already triggered and ready to fight. If we give attention to whatever accusation or judgement is being thrown at us we enter the fight zone.

If we let it roll off our back, and just focus on why they might be saying these things we will avoid an argument while still communicating.

After many missed opportunities, eventually I reached a place where I was ready to apply it in the heat of the moment with easily one of the most challenging persons I could, my own mother.

I remember it clearly. I was home for the holidays and hadn't seen my family in over a year and we were having a good time. And then, in my opinion at the time, my Mom started going off the handle once again, misconstruing what I said and taking it personally. I was feeling immediately exasperated and annoyed and was ready to start the whole painful process of arguing with someone I love when I remembered, *"Oh yeah! Emergency Empathy!"*

My first thought after remembering emergency Empathy was, *"Man I don't want to guess how she feels right now."* My blood was already boiling and I was feeling combative, ready to point out to her all the ways I thought she was being unreasonable.

Instead, I switched gears and tried to think of how she felt and why. My next thought was, " *I don't know why she is acting like this!*" And then I remembered, oh yeah, I don't have to be correct. I just have to be genuinely asking.

So I made a stab in the dark and said,

"Are you feeling annoyed because you think I was implying that you were responsible for the argument during dinner last night?"

It felt so awkward and weird to make this statement in that moment because I was pretty certain this was not the reason she was so upset but I had to say something. It almost felt like I was speaking a foreign language. I had very little faith that it would work in that moment but to my surprise I could see her get a little bit calmer as she answered.

"No I had nothing to do with that so I don't even know why you are bringing it up."

I said,

"Ok, are you feeling upset because you think I don't care about how you feel?"

I had no idea if I was correct or not but my intention was to genuinely connect and again she got a little calmer as she corrected me.

"No I'm sick and tired of being blamed for everyone else's attitude problems!"

I said,

"So you're feeling angry because you feel like you get blamed for things that aren't your fault?""

She said, *"Yes! I'm Angry. I'm angry! I'm angry for everyone blaming me all the time! All I ever try to do is just help and no-one appreciates it."*

When she made that last statement the energy immediately shifted in the room. She relaxed even more and then was basically calm and quiet for a moment ready to hear what I had to say. She felt heard and understood and was ready to have a back and forth conversation again.

A minute before that she wasn't listening to anything I had to say and was vacillating between tears and rage and now after just a few rounds of Emergency Empathy she was calmly ready to talk and listen.

Five minutes later we were back to laughing and having a good time whereas the usual pattern would have been hours or days of fighting and hurt feelings before the energy was resolved.

This is the power of **Emergency Empathy**. It can literally take an argument or fight and rapidly de-escalate it into a productive communication filled with connection and understanding. I promise you it really works, but like all the steps of NVC, doing it correctly takes vigilance and practice.

One common mistake I see, even from experienced NVC users is that instead of asking if someone feels a certain way, they project the feeling onto them.

For example

"You seem angry" **(projecting)** as opposed to *"are you angry because...?"* **(Asking)**

"You seem angry" can easily be received as if you are trying to put them in a box and generally no one is going to like that whether it is correct or not. Asking

them if they are angry and why they might feel that way allows them to be the authority on their inner state instead of you.

Some more examples are

"You are clearly upset...." **(telling)** as opposed to *"Are you upset because....."* **(asking)**

"You look worried...." **(analyzing)** as opposed to *"Are you worried because..."* **(asking)**

This is a small adjustment but can make a world of difference on how effective the technique can be in calming an intense and combative interaction.

Another potential pitfall to be avoided when using **Emergency Empathy** is throwing in a subtle judgement or criticism when guessing why they feel the way they do.

For example, *"Are you angry because you are too insecure to trust anybody?"* As opposed to something like, *"Are you angry because you think I'm being dishonest?"*

It's important to remember you don't have to be correct. Far better to be incorrect than to throw in a not so subtle insult or judgement, which would be much more likely to be used as the stimulus for more anger instead of creating more connection.

Understanding the technique is the first step to using NVC but implementing it into your daily life is likely to require considerable focus and diligent practice. Emergency Empathy is incredibly powerful when used correctly and at the right time. Mistakes will be made so be easy on yourself and continue working at it to make it second nature.

To me it feels almost magical whenever I remember to use it and see how quickly it diffuses a combative interaction and intensely frustrating when I realize I completely forgot to use it and went ahead and had an argument.

NVC is similar to martial arts in that, most of the time you don't really need it but every once in a while it can come in amazingly handy.

Chapter 8

When to use NVC

When you are hanging out and having a good time with your friends, it is unnecessary to focus on using proper NVC, though it still has it's place. As soon as some form of tension arises between you and another, the true usefulness of NVC will shine.

It may happen that we get slightly annoyed about something and think it is better to let the moment pass without saying anything to keep the peace. The challenge with this method is the feeling of annoyance came up for a reason and ignoring it will not make it go away. The feeling will just get stored in your body somewhere and combine with other suppressed feelings of annoyance until it eventually comes out in your tone, attitude, or some form of passive aggressive communication.

When I first learned NVC I was working closely with someone for 40 hrs a week continually for over 6 months. I would often get slightly annoyed but figured there was no point in bringing it up all the time and decided to choose my battles carefully and rarely said anything directly.

After several months of this it built up to such a point that I was getting intensely annoyed many times a day and it was not proportionate to what had occurred because I had so much backlogged unexpressed emotion. We eventually stopped working together and never had a chance to repair our relationship even though we tried several times. I had let it get way too far.

If I had honored and expressed my feelings using NVC as they came up we could have continued to have a healthy friendship. Instead we barely talk because there is still a bunch of unresolved issues and we no longer work together.

To honor how we feel is to accept and express each emotion when it arises in us. Yes, mistakes will be made but you will learn and succeed faster if you allow yourself to make more mistakes. Mistakes are the seeds of wisdom.

Since how you feel will inevitably come out sooner or later, it is more productive to address things as they come up than to put them off indefinitely. Some people are afraid that if they bring up every time they feel annoyed with someone there will be no time for anything else.

On the other hand, we often get annoyed at different times for the same core reason even though it may be through different circumstances.

For example, say you have a need for a level of respect that is frequently not met by a coworker and throughout the day you feel annoyed. You may think to yourself. *"I don't want to bring this up again and again all the time. I'd have no time for anything else."*

However, if you bring it up and use proper NVC then it is more likely to get resolved completely and than there won't be fifteen other times in the day when you get annoyed from dealing with the same underlying unresolved issue.

Let's say Jorge gets annoyed every time his wife Sasha tries to make a decision for him, and it happens often. Jorge may think if he brought it up every time it happened they would be arguing all day. She tries to tell him what to wear, what to eat, what toothpaste to use, when to sleep, etc. He gets a little annoyed each time but never says anything and it just builds and builds creating more distance between them.

If Jorge brought it up the first time it happens in the day using proper NVC, then they may resolve the issue for good.

(fact) *"Honey, when you just said I should wear the blue jeans because I look silly in my black ones* **(feeling)** *I felt annoyed* **(need)** *because I like to make my own decisions about my wardrobe.* **(Request)** *Would you be willing to not offer me advice on my clothing choices unless I ask for your opinion?"*

This would be a proper NVC opening statement that could lead to a deeper realization they have some significant trust issues that need to be worked out or something along those lines. If they are able to use proper NVC and Emergency Empathy to get to the root of these issues and uncover what both their needs are, they may be able to resolve it completely. Once it is resolved, it doesn't need to be worked on anymore and their relationship can continue to grow and deepen.

If Sasha immediately got defensive and triggered at Jorge despite his proper NVC technique, then Emergency Empathy could be applied until she felt heard and they could resume communicating in a conscious way.

His willingness to bring it up even though it might have seemed small and silly is what gives them the opportunity to work it out. If he didn't bring it up, all he is doing is delaying the inevitable because his annoyance will soon leak out one way or another.

Every minor annoyance leads to a deeper fundamental issue if you follow it back to its source. Every issue is waiting to be worked out to experience the full potential of a relationship.

Eventually all the major issues can get resolved and you can enter into a new stage of the relationship. A stage of stability and peace where you both understand how to make things work without compromising what's important to you.

In summary, it is important to honor your unpleasant feelings every time they arise especially within the context of an important relationship. If you are willing to bring attention to and talk about any issue that comes up in a nonviolent way, eventually all of the major issues will get the chance to be resolved and a relationship will truly flourish.

Bringing up minor annoyances may feel unnecessary or tedious in the moment but I promise you the result will be a deeper and more profound relationship filled with authenticity, love, connection and understanding.

Chapter 9

Guiding Principles

Facts, Feelings, Why, and Specific Requests

Feelings matter.

We are all responsible for how we feel.

Nobody wants to be criticized, judged, guilt tripped, labeled, or told they are bad and wrong in any way.

Opinions, evaluations, and judgements are not helpful to resolving conflicts.

Emergency Empathy works-(guess how they feel and why)

Feelings are generally one word.

If you are expressing a feeling in a sentence that starts with "I feel as if..." or "I feel like..." it's most likely some form of analysis, diagnosis, judgement, or guilt trip and not a feeling.

Questions are often less triggering than statements.

Mistakes lead to wisdom.

Chapter 10

NEEDS

CONNECTION	SAFETY	TRUTH	JOY	FREEDOM
acceptance	alignment	authenticity	Art	adventure
affection	awareness	clarity	beauty	choice
appreciation	balance	honesty	celebration	contribute
alliance	competence	genuineness	enthusiasm	creativity
belonging	consistency	integrity	excitement	discovery
closeness	consciousness	knowledge	exercise	experiment
cooperation	direction	learning	fulfillment	explore
community	fairness	presence	generosity	expression
communication	fidelity	purpose	growth	independence
companionship	guidance		harmony	learn
compassion	help		happiness	movement
consideration	intelligence		health	to make noise
consciousness	loyalty		humor	options
contribution	order		inspiration	preference
empathy	peace		music	space
friendship	presence		passion	spontaneity
intimacy	punctuality		play	take risks
kinship	quiet		pleasure	to speak
love	reliability		purpose	
nurturing	respect		Quiet	
participation	rest		relevance	
sexual expression	security		relaxation	
touch	shelter		stimulation	

to be seen	stability			
to be heard	support			
touch	trust			
understanding				
union				
warmth				

Chapter 11

Negative Feelings List

A	B	C	D	E
ashamed	bored	cold	down	enraged
awkward	belligerent	claustrophobic	dazed	exasperated
antsy	bad	cranky	doubtful	exhausted
alarmed	bitter	concerned	dumbfounded	embarrassed
annoyed	blue		dismal	
anxious	bummed		depressed	
apprehensive	broken		dejected	
angry			distressed	
adrift			despondent	
agitated			disconsolate	
awful				
			discouraged	
			dismayed	
			disturbed	
			disjointed	

F	G	H	I	J
furious	gloomy	heated	ill	jittery
fiery	glum	hot	ill tempered	jumpy
fierce	grief-stricken	heartbroken	impassioned	
forlorn		heartsick	indignant	
frightened		heavy hearted	irate	
flustered		heavy	irritable	
freaked out		horrified	incensed	
		hostile		

L	M	N	O	P
low	mad	nervous	outraged	pessimistic
lethargic	melancholy	numb	out of sorts	pensive
lost	mournful	naked	overwhelmed	perplexed
lonely	morbid	neutral		petrified
leery	morose			perturbed
				preoccupied

Q	R	S	T	U
queasy	rattled	sore	turbulent	unhappy
	restless	stupid	troubled	upset
		stunned	timid	unconnected
		surly	terrified	uncomfortable
		suspicious	tense	uneasy
		sorry		unhinged
		sorrowful		unsettled
		scared		unsafe
		shocked		
		spooked		
		startled		
		sheepish		
		self conscious		
		stressed		

V	W			
vexed	wrathful			
vulnerable	worried			
	wistful			

Made in the USA
Middletown, DE
01 July 2025